WHAT YOUR TUTOR MAY NEVER TELL YOU

A Guide for Medical Students
in Problem-Based Learning

Revised Edition

by

Howard S. Barrows MD

Southern Illinois University

School of Medicine

Copyright © 1996

Board of Trustees of Southern Illinois University

All rights reserved. This book or parts thereof, may not be
reproduced in any form or by any means, electronic or
mechanical including photocopy, recording, or any information
storage and retrieval system now known or to be invented,
without written permission from the publisher, except in the
case of brief quotations embodied in critical articles or reviews.

Published by
Southern Illinois University School of Medicine
Springfield, Illinois

ISBN - 0-931369-29-0
Library of Congress (Requested)
First Edition

Revised Edition published 1997

ACKNOWLEDGMENTS

I would like to thank Andrea Lee and Julie Lund, students in the PBL Curriculum who made me realize the need for this book. I am also indebted to them as well as PBL students Marcia Sawa and Nicole Webel for taking the time from their busy lives as medical students to carefully review this booklet from the student point of view. They made many valuable suggestions for improvement.

I am indebted to Linda Distlehorst, Jaime Estavillo, Earl Loschen, Walter Myers, Julie Robbs and Sandra Shea for their many helpful suggestions from the point of view of teaching faculty. I am also indebted to David Wade for his many suggestions to improve this revised edition.

Table of Contents

INTRODUCTION

There are a number of books on problem-based learning written for teachers, including a book on how to be an effective tutor. However, this book is written expressly for medical students. It is long overdue as PBL is a student-centered educational method in which you become responsible for your own learning.

Much of the power behind PBL as an educational method lies in the discussions you and your group have as you work with a patient problem and study together. You express your ideas, discuss the ideas of others, ponder unclear issues and different points of view, go after references, pick the brains of faculty, and learn from and help each other.

In PBL you learn as you work with actual patient problems like those you are going to face in the future as a physician. You are able to practice your problem-solving and self-directed learning skills. In PBL you can see to it that everything you learn is relevant to preparing for your career as a physician.

The steps you go through in the PBL learning process simulate the same process you will use in your future work as a physician. Physicians encounter their patients as an unknown, without prior preparation, and have to evaluate and initially manage the patient problem with the knowledge and skills they already possesses at the time. They then have to get whatever additional information is necessary to fully understand and manage the patient's problem, using resources in their office, the library, computer-mediated searches, talking with consultants. They then apply what was learned in the continuing management of the patient. In all of this the physician needs to be aware of how well they are meeting the needs of their patients and how well they are keeping up with their particular field of medicine. This is exactly the sequence of events you carry out with each patient problem in PBL.

In addition to following a basic sequence of clinical behaviors, PBL stimulates you to learn what is relevant in the basic sciences of medicine while you practice and perfect the clinical skills you will need for your work as a clinical clerk and subsequently as a physician during internship, residency and practice.

The PBL process also has little tricks thrown into it that have been learned from the basic sciences of education, cognitive science and educational psychology. The results of research into the reasoning process of the physician, how to encourage the understanding, retention and application of knowledge, and the importance of student-centered learning have all informed and further shaped the PBL process. This is why tutors function as a guide and not as a dispenser of knowledge, as that would make you dependent on their expertise instead of being an independent thinker who can find the facts needed from experts around the world. Knowledge that you realize you need, that you dig out on your own and apply to a patient problem is better remembered and more useful to future clinical work than knowledge given in a lecture or in assigned reading. Other subtle twists in the PBL process that work towards building your skills as a physician will be mentioned later in the description of the process itself.

However, for you to maximize on the advantages of PBL as an educational method the process described here has to be followed in detail and in sequence. This book was created to put you more in control of the PBL process by understanding the rationale for each step and working with your tutor to be sure that the process will maximize your learning.

Every step in the PBL process is designed with your future role as a physician in mind. Each step has you carrying out a task that will be required in your career as a physician and will best ensure that what you learn will be retained, recalled and applied to your work with patients. Knowing how each step in the process should be carried out and its relationship to your evolving skills as a physician will allow you to use the process fully and its value to your own learning in PBL will be enhanced.

In the "Further Reading" section at the end, related books on PBL are listed.

STARTING WITH A NEW GROUP

There are some routine steps that should be taken when you meet with a new group and tutor.

Introductions

Everyone needs to introduce themselves. Each person should tell the new group where they are from and where they went to college or university before medical school, any interesting work or studies and interests pursued outside of medicine. Each should describe their anticipated career in medicine even if it seems a long way off and minds may change many times. You will usually find some in the group have fairly strong ideas about the career they want to pursue in medicine.

These introductions allow you to become familiar enough with each other to begin working as a team. You'll find some members that have unusual backgrounds and some that may have interests similar to yours.

All of you in the group will be able to get an idea about areas of expertise in the group, which can be useful in working through problems later.

Be sure tutors introduce themselves as well.

In your medical career you will frequently find yourself in a task force, committee or health care team; introductions allow you to know where everyone fits in and facilitates a productive work environment.

Climate Setting

Express your ideas and thoughts freely!

The learning atmosphere or climate in PBL is dramatically different from anything you may have encountered in your prior educational experiences. First of all, get over any concern that you shouldn't volunteer an opinion unless you know for sure that you are right. Your hunches, guesses and ideas are needed.

In PBL it is actually wrong to keep your ideas and thoughts to yourself, even if you're not sure you're right. In PBL it is essential that you express your thoughts about the problem you are working on through the ongoing discussions and comments made within the group. It makes no difference how way out they might seem to others. Expressing your ideas and knowledge gives you a chance to articulate your thoughts in the group, to get their reactions or thoughts and to clarify or improve your own thinking. You can always qualify your ideas with a statement such as "I am not sure of this, but I think...," etc. If you don't share your ideas because you fear they might be wrong you may deprive the group of the correct answer because your hunch, no matter how off-base or preposterous it may seem, might actually be the right answer. Speaking up allows the group to benefit from your thinking and for you to benefit from the group's thinking. Later on, as you work with the problem (especially after self-directed study) you will be able to reinforce, modify or correct your ideas. The silent member of the group does not help himself or the group.

Comment on the ideas and opinions of others

If you have a different opinion than that expressed by someone in the group, a different point of view or facts that differ from those expressed you must speak up. In this way all the members of the group can benefit from the knowledge and thoughts of each other.

It would be a great waste of time if after every idea expressed by someone in the group, the tutor would have to ask each of you if you agree with what was said. It should be a rule that if someone says something and no one in the group speaks up, they all must agree with what was said. This rule does not hold for the tutor. Tutors may disagree with you and not say anything.

The role of the tutor

Be sure your tutors describe their role in the group during the climate discussions.

Tutors are there to stimulate and guide discussion. They are not to be a source of information about any aspect of the problem, even if they are experts. Tutors do not teach in the conventional sense of the word, nor convey to anyone that they agree or disagree with what is being said. However, they actively guide the process of PBL through questions aimed at provoking your thinking and discussions such as: "What's going on with this patient?" "What ideas do you have?" "What do we need to find out about the patient to support those ideas?" The tutor should constantly challenge you about your thinking to be certain how well you know or understand what you are talking about, what the terms you use mean, and that you are carrying your thinking down to basic science mechanisms and concepts. To do this the tutor may need to ask "Why?" again and again, almost ad nauseam. The tutor does most of the questioning in this way initially, but as the unit progresses this is the responsibility of the students. By questioning each other and asking "why" students must be thinking constantly and analyzing the problem.

A major objective of the tutor is to eventually become un-necessary as all the group takes increasing responsibility for keeping track of the PBL process and challenging each other with "Why?", "What is your evidence for that idea?" etc. etc. Tutors then need to comment only when they feel it is necessary.

The tutor can be thought of as an educational coach. Instead of being a "sage on the stage" as in conventional teaching the tutor is a "guide on the side."

Don't panic! There are many faculty available to you who are willing and able to give you information when you want it. There are faculty whose role is to give freely of their expertise and to provide information when you ask for it. They are usually called "resource faculty" and you will see them listed in the guide you receive with every unit. Actually, they are best thought of as "consultants," as they are experts in disciplines related to the problems you will be working with. They are prepared to give you whatever information you are looking for, suggest references and answer your questions. From now on they will be called consultants in this book.

You are certainly free to go beyond the listed consultants. You will find that most of the school's faculty are willing consultants when approached.

Your own role and responsibility

You and your group must take on increasing responsibility for the PBL process and your own learning. You are all expected to accept more and more responsibility for your own thinking and learning, for the PBL process itself and the group's activities and tasks. You should make the tutor unnecessary!

Establishing a similar climate is essential in any working group in your medical career. It facilitates team work and sets the stage for group members to learn from each other.

STARTING WITH A PROBLEM

Setting Objectives

Your group needs to agree on the learning objectives to be addressed with each problem. At first, this may seem like an artificial process. However, it will become both easier and more meaningful with each patient problem you undertake. The setting of learning objectives resolves a number of concerns.

- One patient problem could lead to many months of study if you were to understand all possible aspects of the problem such as: basic science issues from molecules up through cells, tissues and organs (biochemistry, physiology, anatomy, pharmacology, immunology, microbiology and pathology etc.); the mechanisms producing clinical symptoms and signs; clinical skills needed for diagnostic workup and treatment; epidemiological, economic and sociological aspects of the problem, etc. etc. You will need to focus on the areas of most importance to you and your group.

- Each of you comes to medical school with different back- grounds, areas of strengths and weaknesses related to your preparation for medical school. And each comes with different interests in medicine. It is important that your own problem-related study, which is under your control in PBL, is tailor-made to your personal educational needs and desires.

- Every section of the medical school curriculum has a different emphasis. In the first two years it is hoped you will build a firm foundation in the normal form and function of the body as well as the mind and the mechanisms involved in disease processes. This should then prepare you for the last two clinical years applying that foundation to the analysis and management of patient problems. Depending on where you are in a PBL curriculum you need to agree on the areas of learning that will receive emphasis.

- As you progress with problems in a unit, you may notice that your learning has concentrated more on some disciplines and others have been neglected. When this happens you will need to agree to an increased emphasis on these areas with subsequent problems.

You and your group need to decide on the learning objectives you will concentrate on in your problem work. There usually are unit guides in the curriculum to help you in your deliberations.

Once agreed upon, the objectives serve as a guide to your problem work. If you are concentrating on basic science objectives, your hypotheses about the causes for the patient problem and your learning issues should reflect this emphasis.

The objectives also serve as a monitor of your progress. For example, a group that has agreed on basic science objectives may become involved in the clinical aspects of the patient's problem and may want to provide urgently needed care instead of continuing with discussions of basic science issues. Someone in the group (often the tutor initially) may note that the group's discussion and concerns are traveling down a different road or becoming tangential to where the group intended to go. The objectives agreed upon will allow the group to decide where they should be going.

It is OK to alter learning objectives and make mid-course corrections, but they should always be a current guide to where the group intends to go with the problem.

Presenting The Problem

The patient problem can be encountered in a variety of simulation formats, each with particular educational advantages and disadvantages.

The Problem-Based Learning Module (PBLM)

Most of the problems you will be working with in your study

will be in the form of PBLMs. These are printed patient
simulations that are based on real patients and designed to
allow you to ask the patient any question you would like on
history, perform any item of the physical examination and order
any laboratory or diagnostic test, all in any sequence you wish,
just as you are able to do in the real clinical setting. The PBLM
will give you the patient's answers to your questions and will
describe what you would find on any item of physical
examination you choose to perform as well as the results of the
laboratory and diagnostic tests you order. Whatever you can do
to the actual patient in an initial workup you can do to the
PBLM.

After you have made decisions about the PBLM patient you can
then follow the patient's actual course in the patient progress
section, with the care provided by those responsible for the
patient.

The PBLM reader

One member in the group will need to take the PBLM and read
the patient's responses to questions, examinations and the
results of laboratory and diagnostic tests. The reader
represents the patient for the group. It is important that the
reader does not provide answers to questions and results of
examinations accidentally seen while searching through the
pages of the PBLM, things that were not asked for by the
group.

The PBLM User Guide

There is a "User Guide" that comes with the PBLMs (the same
User Guide can be used with any PBLM). It lists all the
questions (Q series), items of examination (E series) ,
laboratory and diagnostic tests (T series) by code numbers.
With these numbers, the PBLM reader is able to turn to the
appropriate patient response in the PBLM. Every member in
the group should have a copy of this guide to refer to in
problem-solving discussions. It is important not to "window
shop" through this booklet, but rather follow your own line of
investigation as you reason through the patient problem. In

other words, find questions that match your thoughts, instead of the other way around. You won't have such a menu in front of you with a real patient, and you need to ask and examine relative to your hypotheses about the patient's problem.

The scribe and the board

One member takes on the task of the "scribe," recording the group's work with the patient, ideas about the problem, the facts the group discovers about the patient, and the learning issues that need to be addressed during self-directed study time. The scribe should divide a blackboard or marker board (from now on referred to as the "board") into four columns. The title "Hypotheses" should be at the top of the first column. At the top of the next "Facts." At the top of the third "Learning Issues." And over the fourth "Actions." The reasons for these columns will become apparent as the PBL process is described.

All of these tasks are rotated among group members with subsequent problems.

The Sequential Problem Simulation (SPS)

The SPS is a simpler format that presents the patient problem in logical segments or installments. This format also requires a reader and scribe with similar roles as in the PBLM. After the reader has read the first installment, usually containing the presenting picture of the patient and some initial information, the group discusses the facts they feel should be recorded by the scribe, their hypotheses, and what further information they would need to narrow down on these hypotheses. After they have carried out discussions as far as feasible, the reader then presents the next installment providing more information about the patient problem and the discussions continue as with the PBLM.

With the SPS format the members of the group cannot get the answers to the particular questions they would have liked to ask the patient in the previous installment or the findings on items of physical examinations they would have liked to perform in the previous installment. You cannot carry out a free inquiry related to hypotheses entertained. Each subsequent installment may provide some of those answers and findings within the other information provided.

The advantage to the SPS is that it is easy to create and takes less time to work through in the group. The disadvantages are that it does not allow you to practice and develop your clinical reasoning skills as is possible with the PBLM, it does not have the same richness of information, and it does not give you a feeling of responsibility for resolving the patient problem. The latter may have a lot to do with the power of the PBL process.

The Standardized Patient (SP)

These are non-patients who have been carefully trained to simulate an actual patient on history and physical, with a reality that often cannot be detected by skilled clinicians. On a number of occasions they will be available for you to use in your problem work. Every curricular unit has a number of problems that can be encountered first as a SP. They can be scheduled through the curriculum coordinator to be available to your group. With the SP you can learn, practice and perfect your history taking skills, physical examination skills, communication and interpersonal skills while you tackle the patient problem. Usually there is a PBLM associated with each SP allowing you to order laboratory and diagnostic tests after you have examined the SP and to follow the patient's course.

An interviewer, an examiner, (and an educator)

Usually a member of the group (in rotation) will take on the principal responsibility for interviewing the patient and another for the examination. During the interview and examination group discussion is possible at any time by using the "time out - time in" technique. When "time out" is called (often by the tutor, but you can negotiate this) the SP acts as if not in the room, allowing for free discussion about the problem. When the group is ready to proceed with the problem, "time in" is called and the SP continues as if there was no break. You can talk about things you wouldn't want a real patient to hear. In fact, the "time in - time out" technique allows you to recognize what kinds of things should not be said in front of patients. It is inappropriate in a clinical setting with a patient to use a board with the four columns for discussions, as is done with the PBLM. Instead, each member of the group should keep personal notes, as occurs in the real clinical situation. When the group has finished the clinical encounter with the SP and returns to their work room for further discussion about the problem, data from members notes can be used to put information in the columns on the board. The PBLM may then be used as the source of continued information about the problem.

It is important to approach the SP as you would an actual patient, dressed appropriately for a patient encounter and acting in a professional manner. This allows you to practice your professional manner and skills as well as your history, physical, communication and interpersonal skills. During "time out" the examiners' skills can be discussed by the group along with the problem being presented by the patient.

Occasionally an actual patient may be available for the group to interview and examine. In this instance the time out - time in procedure would be inappropriate and you will have to save your comments and your thinking about the patient problem until after the patient has left the room. However, it would be appropriate for others in the group to be able to ask questions of the patient after the history has been taken by one member of the group and to do other items of the physical examination when the group member doing the physical examination has finished. This allows all in the group to carry out an inquiry that will satisfy the ideas or hypotheses each may have in their own minds. Why all these things were done can be discussed afterwards.

These inquiry-based problem formats (PBLM and SP) allow you to interact with a real patient problem that presents as it would in a physician's practice. Each allows you to practice and perfect your reasoning skills as you inquire freely about the patient problem (history, physical, tests) in the manner you feel appropriate. In addition, the SP allows you to practice and perfect your clinical, communication, interpersonal and professional skills.

Assigning Tasks

Before the group starts with the problem in the PBLM format someone should volunteer to be the scribe and another to be the reader. In preparation to record the group's thinking the scribe needs to divide the board into the four areas described earlier.

The task of the scribe is difficult. The scribe has to accurately record what the group is thinking in the appropriate columns and at the same time be an active, participating member of the group.

If the group is starting with a SP (or patient), one member should volunteer to take the history and another to do the physical examination. It is sometimes valuable for another member to volunteer to provide the patient with feedback about what the group has decided with regard to diagnosis and management. In addition, they can provide any explanations that are needed to ensure the patient understands and will comply with the treatment plan (patient education). After the group has dismissed the SP they should return to work with the board.

These assigned roles should be rotated so that every member has a chance to carry out these tasks.

Reasoning Through The Problem

The following activities should be undertaken with every problem. They parallel those you will use with patients in your medical practice. This is the great power of PBL; it has you practicing and perfecting the very skills you will need in medical practice as you learn. The relevance of each step to your evolving skills as a physician will be described; many of these activities described below will recycle during your problem-solving process.

Once the patient's problem or complaint is presented (read from the PBLM, presented by the SP) the group should think of the possible hypotheses that could explain the patient's problem and list them on the board. Hypotheses are conjectures, ideas, guesses about what could explain the patient's problem.

Under the Facts column on the board, the scribe should list the facts from the patient presentation that the group feels are important to record (patient's complaints, age, sex, appearance, etc.).

Sometimes the patient's complaint, as presented, may be vague and suggest innumerable hypotheses (such complaints as fatigue, headache, abdominal pain, etc.), and you may want to ask a few questions of the patient to better focus on the nature of the complaint before listing all the hypotheses you can think of that could be responsible.

Hypothesis generation

Hypothesis generation is a creative, mind-stretching activity and is essential in determining the kinds of information you need to obtain from the patient to narrow down on the correct hypothesis. Everyone's ideas should be listed in the Hypotheses column, no matter how unlikely or remote they may seem. They do not need to be listed in any particular order initially as the list can be tidied later.

When a hypothesis is suggested, the person who suggested it should describe what he knows about the entity hypothesized (disease, disease process, syndrome, physiological or anatomical dysfunction, etc.) and why it seems to explain the patient's problem. Hypotheses could be descriptions of defects such as: the patient is not absorbing nutrients or the patient's liver is not making enough albumin. Hypotheses can just be hunches, based on little specific knowledge, but the person making it needs to describe what he knows about that hypothesis. Others in the group have the responsibility of commenting if they would define the entity hypothesized differently or disagree about its ability to explain the patient problem as presented. Hypothesis generation can be facilitted by each student writing down his or her own hypotheses on a piece of paper prior to an open discussion. If the hypothesis suggested is not clearly understood, or if there is disagreement about it, the scribe should be asked to list what needs to be learned on the board under the Learning Issues column. That column does not need to be tidy or neat either, it can be cleaned up when more is known or understood. If the group has agreed on basic science objectives, the learning issues should be stated to reflect the need to acquire a basic science understanding.

ADVICE TO QUIET MEMBERS IN A GROUP

Not everyone speaks their mind freely in group discussions. Some are naturally taciturn or reserved in manner and reluctant to join in discussions. This quality, admirable in many situations, is counterproductive in PBL. It is the different experiences, knowledge and ways of thinking within the group applied in active discussions that makes PBL a powerful learning method! If you are quiet during group discussions, the members of the group cannot profit from your own knowledge, experience and ideas.

If you don't express your own thinking and understanding, you miss the opportunity to have the accuracy or validity of your ideas tested in the group's discussion. Speaking up in the group is also a valuable way to learn how to communicate to others and to use correct medical language.

A more serious problem posed by the quiet group member is that the tutor and the other members of the group can never be sure how well you understand what is going on in the group's discussions or how much you have learned.

One reason for quietness is that you feel you don't know enough to contribute. No one in the group can take the risk of having quietness misinterpreted. The quiet, non-contributing student survives poorly in the clinical clerkships where quietness is interpreted as ignorance. In the clinical clerkships the measure of a student's understanding and knowledge is based in a large part on active discussions with clinical faculty in seminars and rounds.

Therefore, if you are quiet you must recognize this and force yourself to deliberately and regularly contribute to group discussions. If you find this difficult, and many do, especially in a group of very talkative students, you should discuss this during the group's assessment session at the end of the problem (see below). Perhaps a contract can be made with your colleagues that they will pause frequently in ongoing discussions and ask for your opinion.

Inquiry And Analysis

Once the group has listed all the possible hypotheses they can think of with the patient problem, they should ask the patient the questions they feel will help establish or rule out the hypotheses listed. With each question suggested, if it is not obvious to the group, the person suggesting it should be asked to describe the rationale for the question in relationship to the hypotheses on the board. This inquiry, to verify or rule out hypotheses, is a deductive logical reasoning skill you will also need to perfect, in contrast to the free creative, inductive reasoning used in hypothesis generation.

The new facts learned from the patient's answers need to be analyzed against the hypotheses being considered and what is known about the problem. The information that seems significant, should be recorded by the scribe under Facts. The members of the group should help the scribe decide on what does and does not need to be recorded on the board. The scribe cannot transcribe everything the patient says on the board, only the essentials need to be recorded. This is a skill you will need in your clinical work. You can't remember and record everything you learn during a history and physical examination, you have to decide on what is important and worth recording. Using an organization for the facts you learn about the patient that is similar to that found in practice (chief complaint, history of present illness, past medical history, family history etc.) will help you to become familiar with how to write up your patients in your clinical work.

As the accumulated facts you have learned about the patient on history and physical examination grow in number in the Facts column, a picture of the patient is assembled similar to the picture (or representation) of patients you will have to assemble in your own mind as you work with patients in the future. As the facts grow in the Facts column, you may have to help the scribe reorganize them into a cohesive picture of the patient.

The activities associated with deciding on what questions to ask, reviewing the possible significance of the patient's answers to questions, and the related group discussions, often stimulated by the tutor's questions, will often raise additional unanswered questions about what is going on with the problem and the mechanisms responsible. What anatomical areas, physiological mechanisms, biochemical or molecular derangements are responsible? The group's discussions will reveal areas of disagreement or limited understanding. You have to become sensitive to when this occurs and recognize that it indicates your own and the group's areas of limited knowledge or confusion. It is important to be able to identify these areas and have the scribe list them on the board under Learning Issues.

Problem Synthesis

At some point, after a number of questions have been asked and the group seems to be running out of ideas about what more should be asked, one member of the group should summarize the important facts that have been learned about the patient to that point, without looking at the board. This is an essential skill you will all have to have in your clinical work, on rounds, conferring with colleagues, working with consultants, and writing up your patient in the chart. The rest of the group should listen to the summary without looking at the board as well. Once the summary is finished, the others should add what they remember and they feel needs to be added. This summary should have all the essential facts (you have to learn to decide what they are) and none of the unessential facts about the patient. As time goes on, and you gain experience and knowledge, these summaries should become organized into a logical presentation of the patient's problem.

This summary also ensures the group that you all have a similar picture of the patient. The hypotheses listed on the board should be reviewed after the summary to see if any can be eliminated or weakened (drawing a line through them) and if any are being strengthened or confirmed as possibilities (putting a check mark after them). Often this review of the problem will suggest new hypotheses that should have been considered.

This problem synthesis step can be used on a number of occasions; whenever the group needs to summarize and re-evaluate their hypotheses and inquiry and whenever the group seems to be going nowhere, and refocusing and/or redirection are needed.

All members of the group should attempt this synthesis as it is a most important skill in clinical work.

Although most of the above comments were centered around history taking during inquiry, the same activities go on with items of the physical examination. Often, physical examination findings will lead to more questions.

Eventually your group will have gone as far as it can with the patient problem, using your combined knowledge and skills to analyze what is going on with the patient and what can be done about it. You have expanded, revised and focused hypotheses as well as possible, obtained and organized all the facts you feel are relevant about the patient (in light of your hypotheses) and listed all the areas where further learning and study seem appropriate in the Learning Issues column.

THE "COMPLETE" HISTORY AND PHYSICAL

Invariably a concern will eventually be expressed by members in the group that a complete history and physical examination should be carried out on the patient. It is important to recognize that such a concern is unnecessary and actually counterproductive. Anyone (from K through 16) can memorize all the questions you might ask a patient about demographics, past history, family history, habits, occupation and the symptoms that might suggest trouble in the various organ systems (heart, lung, GI, nervous system, musculoskeletal, etc.) and all the things you might do on a complete physical examination (vital signs, heart, lung, abdomen, eyes, ears, nose, throat, neck, etc.). That does not require any clinical problem-solving skill or clinical rigor and logic. In addition, if you spend the time to do this with every PBLM and SP, your sessions will become inordinately long and boring.

The true intellectual, clinical challenge for a physician is to ask those questions and do those items of physical examination that will most directly and effectively sort out the hypotheses entertained and those few other questions and items of physical examination that are needed to scan for trouble in related organs or systems that might logically be involved with the patient.

You will rarely have more than twenty minutes to half an hour in your clinical work with patients to do a history and physical and every question and item on physical exam you carry out has to count. You need the practice now to apply effective clinical reasoning and decide on an inquiry strategy that will allow you to most effectively sort out the hypotheses you have considered. This is often called a "focused history and physical examination."

As you carry out a focused history and physical on problem after problem, you will eventually and automatically develop an awareness of all the questions you might ask a patient and how you would do a complete physical if that were ever required (as in a routine yearly physical examination).

Future Actions
(Laboratory and Diagnostic Tests, Treatment)

At this point you should list in the Action column the
laboratory and diagnostic tests you feel are indicated to further
evaluate the patient problem. As each member of the group
suggests tests, they should describe why the test is important
in relationship to the hypotheses being considered. You should
also describe what actions should be taken to treat the patient
including pharmaceuticals and their rationale in basic science
terms.

Hold Off On Finding The Results Of Laboratory And
Diagnostic Tests Until After Self-Directed Learning

It is tempting to continue with the problem and learn the
results of the tests. However, there are good reasons not to do
this in terms of your own learning. Test results narrow your
hypothesis list and you are less likely to do self-directed
learning on hypotheses that are ruled out by the laboratory
data. You lose the stimulus to study many of the hypotheses
you entertained, to see if the hypotheses indeed fit the patient
problem and to learn more about them as well as the basic
science and clinical mechanisms involved, and how you might
further investigate the problem to establish or deny each
hypothesis. Almost invariably, the hypotheses you consider for
the patient are related to the learning that should occur in the
curricular unit you are in and provide a stimulus for productive
and wider learning. If your study is limited to the specific
diagnoses possible in each case, you have limited the power of
PBL. Self-directed study into the alternative hypotheses your
group considered will give you information that will make you
more effective when those hypotheses need to be considered in
subsequent problems. Also, holding off laboratory tests gives
you the opportunity to see if you chose the right tests and to
learn about others that should have been considered.

The results of tests are usually not available when you order
them anyway.

Commitment As To Probable Outcome

When your group has gone as far as it can with the problem, you each need to make a commitment about what you think will eventually turn out to be the cause of the patient's problem. You should also make a commitment as to what should be done about the problem, and how it should be managed. These commitments should be recorded by the scribe.

Your immediate reaction to this idea will be that you don't have enough information yet to make such a commitment. You feel that you need to look things up, find out more about the patient and tackle some learning issues before you can make any commitment. You can change your mind later on, but make a commitment now! What is needed is your best guess or "gut reaction." What would you bet on, at this point, as the most likely diagnosis and most appropriate treatment?

This commitment does two things of value for you. First, it will further motivate you to look things up during your self-directed study (see below) to see if you are right. Secondly, it prepares you for an important skill you will need in your clinical work the rest of your life. There will be many times that you will feel you would like to have more information about a patient's problem but it is just not available and you will have to make a decision anyway and act on it! You can't tell the patient, especially in an urgent situation, that you don't know what is going on and you will have to come back when you have more information. Decision making with inadequate data, when no more is available at the time, is an important skill.

Learning Issues Shaping/Assignment

At this point you have come as far as is feasible with your patient's problem, using your own and your group's pooled knowledge and reasoning skills to understand:

- What is the problem?
- What is responsible for the problem?
- What might be done about it?

In this process you all have identified:

- Areas of confusion that need to be resolved through research and study.
- Areas where learning is indicated, especially in light of the subject matter of your curricular unit and the objectives developed by your group at the beginning of the problem.

Now it is time to review, clean up and focus the learning issues the group's scribe has written on the board during the heat of the many discussions that ensued as you reasoned through the problem.

There are undoubtedly some learning issues that were put up early in problem work that may no longer be relevant. There may be learning issues that you now realize are not related to the learning that is relevant to the problem or the unit. These can be eliminated if the group agrees.

As you review the list and keep in mind the problem as you have put it together and the hypotheses you have chosen as most likely, other important learning issues will suggest themselves. The commitments you and the others in the group just made may suggest other learning issues. All these should be added.

You will find that some learning issues are too broad in scope and researching them, as written, would involve far more study time than you want to spend. Split them up into better defined subcategories and eliminate the categories that seem less relevant. For example, a disease entity or category of diseases related to a hypothesis on the board could represent extensive study and it would be better to break it down into physiological aspects, anatomical aspects, clinical symptoms and signs, pathology, immunological aspects etc. and choose the most relevant.

Once the learning issues are expanded, pruned and focused, each member of the group should choose those learning issues that they want to pursue. There are some guidelines for making this choice.

- Many of the issues were raised by certain members of the group because of their awareness of a personal learning need or interest in the subject. They are the most motivated to research the issues.
- Each member of the group should choose learning issues that involve an area where they lack sufficient background or knowledge.
- Members of the group should avoid learning issues where they have some background or are particularly well versed. It is a terrible temptation to choose an issue where you are comfortable, as it is easy to get the needed facts quickly and the new facts are understood easily. It is more productive for each individual and the group if everyone chooses areas of educational need.

When the group returns to the problem after self-directed learning, the members of the group with expertise in an area may discuss or comment on the learning of others in these areas. This promotes good discussion and helps validate learning.

Several members of the group may pick the same learning issues and work together in their research and study.

One, or at the very most two, learning issue of general interest or of central importance might be researched by all members of the group. The group should identify these issues and agree upon them. However, such central issues can often contain many sub issues that could be more productively divided and assigned to individual group members.

DIVIDING LEARNING ISSUES

In the beginning there is a tendency for each member of the group to want to take on all the learning issues. Having just come from more traditional learning experiences where teachers have provided them with all that they should know through lectures and reading assignments, PBL students may be uncomfortable with the idea that they have to learn from fellow group members who are learning as they are and dread the possibility of hearing mini-lectures from other students.

Unfortunately, when every member of the group researches all the learning issues listed, learning is broad and superficial. There is little time to investigate learning issues deeply for understanding, to cross check references and resources for opposing points of view, to check on the reliability of resources and to integrate learning with other knowledge. These are skills that are essential to develop in medical practice. Superficial learning defeats one of the most important aspects of PBL, the ability to pursue information and relate it to your own knowledge base so that it is deeply and well understood.

Dividing up the learning issues allows each member of your group to:

- Be well informed in a unique aspect of the problem.
- Concentrate on areas of learning important to their own growth.
- Have an important role in the follow-up discussions of the problem.
- Set up a logical search strategy for information using primary sources (journals, on-line, faculty).
- Sort through relevant and irrelevant resources.

Each member of the group will see the problem from a different perspective. This increases the depth of the group's discussions as opposed to the broad but superficial understanding, and unified point of view, that occurs when all members take on all issues.

In addition you will learn:
- How to effectively inform your peers in a career that will inevitably involve educating health team members and students.

- To challenge and draw out knowledge from people with expertise.

As you will see later, mini-lectures rarely occur as each member's learning is incorporated into an ongoing review and discussion of the problem. Each member of the group is encouraged to provide handouts concerning what they learned during self-study (reprints of articles, text pages, diagrams, personal notes). These are helpful in reviewing a learning issue which you did not cover in depth.

Even though you concentrate on the few learning issues you have been assigned in the group, there is no reason why you cannot briefly review those assigned to others so as to be better prepared to understand the information they bring to the group (if you have the time).

Those who staunchly resist dividing up learning resources invariably change their minds after giving it a fair trial.

Resource Identification

Now that you have identified the learning issues you plan to tackle, the next step is to identify the information resources you plan to use during your self-directed study. There is a wide range of possibilities:

- Textbooks
- Monographs
- Reviews
- Journal articles
- On-line resources such as Medline and the Internet
- Faculty experts (especially those listed as consultants for your curricular unit)
- Experts in the community
- Experts around the world (telephone or Internet)

You need to decide now which resources will give you the best information for the learning issues you have been assigned (the most effective and efficient resources) and describe them to the group. You may try to develop a strategy in your studies such as:

- Getting an overview of the learning issue in a textbook
- Doing a Medline or Internet search to narrow down on particulars or find the latest information
- Going to a faculty resource person to discuss as yet unresolved questions

As each member of the group discusses the resources they plan to use, the others in the group can question the rationale for their strategies or suggest other resources.

All of this activity has great relevance for your career in medicine. Your patients will constantly present problems you have never encountered before. You cannot learn everything there is to know about medicine during medical school; much of what you learn in medical school will become outdated or wrong, and new information is constantly being generated in all fields of medicine. Therefore, you will always need to:

- Recognize when you need to learn more in your work with patients.
- Identify what you need to learn.
- Choose the most effective, efficient and accurate resource to get this information.

Using experts as resources helps prepare you to use consultants effectively in your practice.

Schedule Follow-Up

Your group needs to decide when you should meet to continue with the patient problem. This decision should be based on the amount of time that will be required to find and research the learning issues. All the members of the group and the tutor should get out their calendars and determine when to meet again. (At some schools there is no predetermined schedule for tutorial meetings and you are free to schedule the times best for all of you. In other PBL curricula, this step may not be necessary as the tutorial meetings are scheduled.)

SELF-DIRECTED STUDY

This is your time to dig out the information you need for your assigned learning issues and then to study and explore all the other areas of the problem that might be productive for you. Since you have only a few learning issues you can explore them in depth. Remember as you study to keep the patient problem in mind.

You should develop a strategy for self-study. For example, as described before, you might get an overview of your learning issue from a textbook, then get a more focused review from a monograph, and then delve into particularly difficult or poorly understood areas with journal articles, or talk with an expert consultant (who, besides answering your questions, may give you other references that may be pertinent). These last two are most important to be certain you have the most current and accurate information. The most recent textbook is already three to four years out of date and superficial in its coverage.

In your medical career you will need to be able to find up-to-date references quickly when working with urgent problems or when you have many patients to care for. You should learn to use library, on-line, Internet or consultants effectively. This is the best time to develop your skills in this area with the help of your group and tutor.

Although you have consultants or resource faculty listed as available in your unit, take it upon yourself to find others in the school or community (or world through telephone or Internet) who might be valuable.

Before going to a consultant, be sure you have already done homework in the area of the learning issue. This will allow you to more readily understand the consultant's information, to focus on the areas you are confused about, and to find out the latest information on the subject.

After you have talked with the consultant, verify the answers you have received if you can. It is always a good habit to check up on authorities, not only to verify their ideas, but also to see if there are different opinions.

There are times you will run into conflicting opinions in your study and this gives you the challenge of deciding for yourself. You will need to do this in the care of your patients. Who's opinion will you follow? You will have to learn to evaluate the research methods used and the decisions based on that research. Initially you may have to use consultants to help you in this evaluation.

The members of your group should be encouraged to collaborate on learning issues, working together to get a better understanding through discussion.

During your own self-study you should copy significant articles, diagrams, reference lists, drawings or charts, or your own personal notes, outlines and/or diagrams that you created during your study for each member of the group. This eliminates the need for you to describe in detail what you have learned in group discussions and provides others with references they can refer to later.

You can also bring books back to the group that others might find useful. And sometimes it might be useful to bring an "expert" (from the faculty or community) back to the group to review the group's thinking with the problem and to answer questions.

PROBLEM FOLLOW-UP

Resources Used And Their Critique

The first item of business on your return is to have a discussion about the resources you used during your self-directed study. Each member of the group should briefly describe the resources they said they would use and the resources they ultimately ended up using and why. This is not a discussion about what you learned, but about the resources you used. It should cover any problems encountered with the resources such as:

• Inadequate or superficial information
• Too detailed
• Out of date
• Inaccurate
• Conflicting opinions with different resources
• Difficulty in contacting a consultant

This is an opportunity for the members of the group to discuss how to access appropriate resources in the future for various kinds of learning issues.

As the group becomes more sophisticated with resources, this step also provides an opportunity to discuss how to evaluate the accuracy of information (reputation of authors, research methods used, statistical methods used).

These steps taken together:
• Resource identification
• Self-directed learning
• Resource use and critique
represent the skills you will need to effectively and efficiently continue your own learning throughout your medical career.

There is a truism in medical education that half of what you learn today will be wrong by the time you graduate, and unfortunately you won't know which half it is. To keep up with your chosen field of medicine and to provide the latest and best care to your patients, you must have very well developed, habitual self-directed learning skills.

Reassess The Problem

Now you are better informed about the problem and, just as in your own practice, you need to apply what you learned back to the patient problem.

Review The Hypotheses List

The first thing the group should do at this point is to summarize the patient problem again. The next is to review the Hypotheses list on the board and indicate where changes should be made. What hypotheses should now be eliminated or altered? What new hypotheses should be added? Any suggestion for such changes should be supported with justifications based on the information from self-directed study. Any handouts that were prepared for the group (copies of articles, personal notes etc.) can be distributed. Suggestions for hypothesis changes, hypothesis elimination or new hypotheses should be challenged, questioned and discussed by the group as appropriate. Comments based on self-directed study should be presented in this discussion.

Often these discussions will reveal that more information may be needed from the patient on either history or physical to better consider presently entertained hypotheses or support new hypotheses suggested. This new information should be analyzed and added to the Facts column for a more complete picture of the patient problem.

In this way, the information gained from self-directed study is applied back to the problem in an active, exciting way that enlarges everyone's understanding of the problem and makes the new information memorable for everyone. It is not necessary for any group members to give mini-lectures since all information will come out with discussions around the problem.

As this goes on, everyone in the group should keep an eye on the learning issues and their assignment listed on the board to make certain all members of the group were able to bring forth the fruits of their research. There is nothing more frustrating than to have researched information for the group and then have no opportunity to apply it to the patient problem; everyone loses.

This is a most important and exciting step in PBL, as a number of very important things are occurring:

- You are all able to critique and correct your prior knowledge and understanding on the basis of your new learning.
- You are able to critique your prior reasoning with the problem.
- The facts you learn are associated in your mind with the symptoms, signs and clinical picture of a patient problem. The facts you learn are also enmeshed with the clinical reasoning used in clinical work. All this insures the recall and application of what you have learned in your subsequent work with patients.

Carry Out Laboratory And Diagnostic Tests Requested

The next step is to carry out the laboratory and diagnostic tests you indicated would be needed in your first session with the problem, now modified by what has been brought back from self-directed learning. Each test should be justified in terms of why it should be performed and what will be learned by a positive or negative result that will be of importance in understanding the problem and designing a treatment approach. Once the result is determined, its significance should be discussed.

Final Decisions About The Problem And Its Management

You and the group should come to a final decision about the patient problem and its management before following the patient's progress in the PBLM. There you will see how those responsible for the actual patient problem cared for the patient. If there were different hypotheses entertained, different tests ordered, or a different management plan carried out, the group needs to discuss why and compare it with your own ideas.

Recycling through another self-study period

In this problem reassessment step you need to be aware of new learning issues that may have arisen. There may be new unanswered questions and new learning issues that need to be posted and assigned. This may require an additional self-study period followed by a return to the problem. When you are in a new curricular unit (dealing with new problems in a new area of learning) you may have to do this several times with the initial problems until you get use to new terminology and concepts, and develop a familiarity with the areas involved. Subsequent problems in the unit will require less recycling as your knowledge in the areas of the unit grows.

If there are only a few new learning issues they might be discussed next time just before taking on a new problem.

AFTER THE CONCLUSION OF THE PROBLEM

The steps that follow are often difficult for the members of the group and for the tutor initially.

Knowledge Summary And Abstraction

You may not realize the true extent of what you learn working with each patient problem in PBL. You learn many things that may not come to mind if, at any point, you ask yourself "what have I learned." Your learning will be recalled when you face a similar patient problem through the cues that trigger associations in your mind. But even then, your learning may only be expressed in the knowledgeable actions you take in working with the problem. You might not be able to explain why you are taking such actions or recall the facts that support them. You see this everyday with experienced physicians who take very effective actions (good diagnostic hypotheses, effective focused history and physical examination, shrewd diagnosis and effective management plan) with a patient problem, but cannot explain why those actions were taken. They have good "procedural knowledge."

Ironically, PBL puts you in the reverse situation of students in traditional curricula who have learned much through rote memorization of information from lectures and reading assignments. They can recall all kinds of information when asked questions or given a written test ("declarative knowledge"), but they cannot readily apply that information to patient problems. You may successfully apply what you have learned to patient problems, but you may not be able to answer questions about your actions. It will be to your advantage to be able to do both. The information you learn in PBL will even be of greater value to you in taking written tests and in working with unusual, complex problems if you can both apply it effectively and describe the principles and concepts behind your actions.

This can be accomplished in the PBL process by consciously attempting to describe verbally and graphically what you have learned from your work with the patient problem. The members of the group should, in turn, try to describe:

- What new things were learned working with the problem?
- How this learning has extended knowledge in related subjects (anatomy, physiology, pathology etc.)? "I learned that edema could be caused by defects in the liver, kidney, heart and lymphatics."
- What new concepts have been learned? "The metabolic acidosis of this diabetic patient gave compensation and the significance of the anion gap."
- How learning in this problem relates to what was learned in past problems? "Lesions in the corticospinal tract can present with a variety of signs in different patients."
- How will the things learned with this problem help with future problems? "I realize that jaundice does not have to be present in a patient with hepatitis."

Each student's comments can be followed by questioning and discussion from the group. When this cycle has finished, the group should try and summarize their learning.

This not only helps make your learning declarative, it also makes your learning transferable to other less directly related patient problems in the future.

An effective tool for these discussions in the group is a concept map. On the board, start with the patient's symptoms and work backwards by steps with a flow chart down to the tissue, organ, cellular and molecular events that were causative.

Abstraction and generalization

This step provides you with the opportunity to make valuable generalizations and abstractions about what you have learned with this problem and its relationship to learning with other problems. This can provide you with a vision that integrates your learning in various disciplines. It is these generalizations that professors invariably provide their class in the beginning to give the students the big picture. As it represents the abstractions and generalizations professors have developed after years of experience and work in their chosen field, it is felt to be of great value in understanding their field ("once you under-stand the thalamus you understand the nervous system"), but it is of no value to the beginning students who have not had enough understanding or experience to profit from those words of wisdom.

Here is the point where you and your group can work at your own generalizations and abstractions to help you remember, recall and apply principles and concepts in the future.

You will need to do this in your future practice experiences.

Self, Peer, Tutor And Group Evaluation

At the end of the PBL process each member of the group needs to evaluate their own progress and the progress of the others in three areas.

Self

Reasoning through the patient problem

This skill was challenged in the first session when the patient problem was encountered as an unknown: hypotheses generated, inquiry undertaken (focused history and physical), facts assembled on the board and decisions made. Although it was a group effort, each member of the group must recall and evaluate the quality of their own reasoning.

Digging out information using appropriate resources

This skill is seen in the resources chosen for assigned learning issues, the resources actually used and the critique of resources on return to the second session. Most importantly, the quality and quantity of the information obtained (in the time available), its usefulness to the group and the group member himself, and how effectively it was applied to the problem and presented to the group should be commented on.

Assisting the group with its task

How effective was the individual member as a part of the team working on the problem? Was the group member too quiet or taciturn, too assertive or controlling? Did the member feel he or she took an active role in the problem discussions and carried his or her own weight? Did he or she communicate well? Were there any interpersonal problems with members of the group? Did he or she help others with theirs?

Some groups find one more area to be of value in self-assessment.

Learning progress

Was significant progress made in learning, considering the problems and disciplines involved in the curricular unit?

Peer

The rest of the group needs to comment following each member's self-evaluation. Was it accurate? Do they see that member's performance differently and how so? Would they add to his comments about himself? This is a challenge for each member to provide honest and accurate feedback to peers. Feedback which will be constructive and helpful. Everyone in the group wants to be an effective physician and to do well in his learning. Accurate feedback, positive or negative, is of great value.

It is important when giving feedback to support your comments with examples. It does little good to tell a member in the group, for instance, that he seemed to treat things too superficially or to tell another you felt she was being too critical of the performance of others, without giving examples.

Tutors may also add to the feedback if they feel appropriate comments have not been made by others in the group.

Tutor

Tutors must also evaluate themselves at the end of every problem. They should discuss how they felt they performed in the tutor role facilitating the group's thinking and discussion and guiding the PBL process. Just as with each student's self-evaluation, the students in the group should discuss a tutor's self-evaluation and provide feedback, positive or negative, about their perception of the tutor's performance. This is the only way your tutors can improve their skills.

Group

At the end of this process, the group should also discuss how they feel they are performing as a group and what improvements need to be made.

Self and peer assessment must be done at the end of every problem. Practice in these complex skills is as important as practice in clinical reasoning and self-directed learning. These assessments at the end of each problem are dress rehearsals for the final, formal written report your group must turn in at the end of the unit. This recurrent assessment is essential as it allows the members of the group to correct problems seen in their performance as the group progresses through a unit.

All working groups inevitably develop interpersonal problems as values, personal goals, ease and difficulty of learning in different areas, personality styles, and ways of doing things vary and conflict arises within the group. When these conflicts do arise, they should be discussed openly and frankly. Every member of the group has a responsibility to help resolve these difficulties. It is not just the tutor's job. The members of the group should work smoothly and effectively as a team; they don't necessarily have to like each other.

The value of these skills to your future are immense and may not be fully recognized by you at this point in your career.

You should be able to assess yourself repeatedly and accurately in your work. Are you effective in your clinical or research work? Do you need to learn more? This is essential to keeping up in your work and educating yourself.

You will be in many situations where it will be important to the care of patients to give accurate feedback to colleagues and health team members. You should be able to do it in a way that is constructive, acceptable and effective.

Interpersonal problems will always occur in your future role as a physician on many teams, committees, and working groups. Although you may be with people you don't care for personally, you have to work with them effectively.

SUMMARY

You could not have chosen a more rewarding or effective way to learn in medical school. You learn from the sciences basic to medical practice while developing the skills you will need to use in medical practice. The relevance and importance of everything you learn to your preparation as a physician is obvious. What you learn will be recalled and effectively applied in your clinical work. You are in control of your own learning and you can make it relevant to your own needs and of the highest quality possible.

Outline of the PBL Process with Page References

Starting a new group (1)

Introductions (1)
Climate setting (1)
- Express your ideas and thoughts freely (1)
- Comment on the ideas and opinions of others (2)
- Silence means assent (2)
- The role of the tutor (3)
- Your own role and responsibility (4)

Starting with a problem (5)

Setting objectives (5)
Presenting the problem (6)
- Problem-based learning modules (6)
- Sequential problem simulations (8)
- Standardized patients (9)
Assigning tasks (11)
- The problem reader (7)
- The scribe and the board (8)
The board (keeping track of the group's reasoning and learning needs) (8)
- Hypotheses
- Facts
- Learning issues
- Actions
Reasoning through the problem (11)
- Hypothesis generation (12)
- Inquiry and analysis (14)
- Problem synthesis (15)
- Future actions (laboratory and diagnostic test, treatment) (18)

Commitment as to probable outcome (19)
Learning issue shaping/assignment (19)
Resource identification (23)
Schedule follow-up (24)

Self-directed study (26)

Problem follow-up (28)

Resources used and their critique (28)
Reassess the problem (29)
- Review the hypothesis list and change as appropriate
- Apply new learning to the problem
- Discuss and hand out references and notes
- Carry out laboratory and diagnostic test requested
- Identify new learnijng issues
Recycle through another self-study period (31)
Final decisions about the problem and its management (30)

After the conclusion of the problem (32)

Summarize new knowledge (32)
Abstractions and generalizations (33)
Self evaluation (34)
- Reasoning through the patient problem.
- Digging out information using appropriate resources
- Assisting the group with its task.
- Learning progress.
Peer, tutor and group evaluation (35)

FURTHER READING

The Tutorial Process
by Howard S. Barrows MD
Southern Illinois University School of Medicine
(revised 1992)

This book is a handbook for tutors. If you want to know more about what is expected in their role or would consider being a tutor in the future you might find the book helpful.

Practice-Based Learning: Problem-Based Learning Applied to Medical Education
by Howard S. Barrows MD
Southern Illinois University School of Medicine (1994)

This book will provide more information about many details of PBL.

Developing Clinical Problem Solving Skills
by Howard S. Barrows, M.D. and G.C. Pickell, M.D.
W. W. Norton & Co., Inc. New York, NY (1991)

This book on clinical reasoning skills is written for medical students and describes in more detail how to reason effectively with a patient problem.